ADA GUTIERREZ

Financial Vocabulary for Beginners

Common Vocabulary Words to Develop Financial Literacy

First edition

This book was professionally typeset on Reedsy.
Find out more at reedsy.com

Contents

1

Vocabulary Words

Employment The condition of having paid work. Working for someone else, for which you are paid.

Employer a person, company or organization that employs people.

Self- Employ Is the state of working for oneself rather than employer. Tax authorities will view a person as self-employed when the person chooses to be recognized as such or if the person is generating income for which a tax return needs to be filed. ("Employment - Wikipedia")

Income: you can refer to the money that person or entity received in exchange for their labor or product. For households and individuals in the United States income is defined by tax law as a sum that includes any wage salary. "Three categories of income are of principal concern to taxpayers: Ordinary income, capital gain, and tax-exempt income." ("Income Definition: Types, Examples, and Taxes - Investopedia")

TIME: time is a measure of nonstop consistent change in our surroundings, usually from a specific viewpoint. While the concept of time is self-evident and intuitive, the steady passing of events before our eyes. The orbit of the moon around our planet describing its fundamental nature is much harder to understand. In other words, time is the state of a continuous clock going in front of our eyes and there is no control over it. That is why it is especially important as human beings to be organized and disciplined to optimize every minute in life.

Financially speaking, time has a major impact on an individual. The younger a person is financially educated the more benefits with less stress can be accomplished. An individual that is well prepared to start investing at the age of eighteen has twice as much impact as a person that starts investing at age 25. If an individual starts investing at their 30s or 40s the potential of increasing wealth it's going to be much harder because the money is not going to have time to compound as if these individuals would have started at 18, 20 or even 25 years of age.

Career: is an individual's metaphoric journey through learning, work, and other aspects of life. ("career development Flashcards | Quizlet") There are several ways to define Career and the term is used in a variety of ways. Finding out at a younger age what is the career that an individual wants to do in life it's also a big step in someone's life. And when choosing a career that requires a lot of years in college or university there is a big need for money. If someone is not prepared for such expenses, these individuals will have to look into financing their education with the help of "student loans", but it is also a way to trap them in a rat race. Unfortunately, student loans start charging interest and are offered to students easily, but when they need to pay them back the borrowers are barely graduating and not making money yet. That is why it's crucial to understand the time, money, and energy spent when the decision is made to follow a career path, it is important to study the possibilities and the potential of earnings as soon as possible to not be stuck with a big debt right after accomplishing one of the biggest goals in life.

2

Retirement

Retirement: The stage of one person's life when they choose to leave their work life behind permanently. The act of retiring or leaving a job career or occupation permanently usually because of age. ("Retirement Definition & Meaning | Dictionary.com")

Retirement Plan: A retirement plan refers to financial strategies of saving, investing, and distributing money meant to sustain oneself during retirement. ("Retirement Letter to Customers Samples") Many popular investment vehicles such as individual retirement accounts and 401Ks. These types of accounts allow retirement savers to grow their money with certain tax advantages. These 401K accounts are offer through employers. What 's good about them is that money can be set aside before taxes, especially if you are someone that is already making a higher income. These types of accounts are a benefit for both the employers and the employees. Unfortunately, our taxes are increasing every year and the 401K's carry management fees for the experts that are managing the money that is set aside for investment. The list can go on, that is why it is particularly important to know the basics about investments and to make sure that your account is being managed appropriately to your needs and your lifestyles and plans for when you retire.

Another important thing to know with retirement accounts is the money that you put in cannot be taken out until you're 59 1/2 years old or older to have less penalties or no penalties for withdrawing this money. And even then, you're not exempt from paying taxes out of the money that is being put aside. Again, that is why the investments must be done with an expert to make sure That the strategies that they're using are correct. If not you might end up retiring with way less money than what it was expected on the initial calculations.

Traditional IRA and Roth IRA in Traditional IRA is an account to which you can contribute pretax or after-tax dollars. Your contributions may be tax deductible depending on your situation, it can give you immediate tax benefits. ("What is a Traditional IRA? | Charles Schwab") Refer to the tax laws to see if your salary and wages qualify for this tax benefit. What difference from this IRA to a 401K is that the holder of the IRA individually does your investments. And the money invested in this account is money after taxes, which means you can withdraw at any time without penalties. Ideally, the longer the money sits in the account the more compound interest it will accumulate. One of the cons of this account is that the amount of money that you can invest is limited. In 2023 the total contributions you can make each year to all your Traditional IRA and Roth IRAs cannot be more than $6,500 or **$7500 if you are age 50 or older.**

This is the traditional idea of retiring after a certain age; but retirement comes when your investments and your passive income it is higher than your job paid income, for which you can be sustained for the rest of your life. Experts say that because of inflation and how expensive everything is, people should have multiple sources of income to support their household. And, when it comes to retiring, also make sure to have not only a 401K or Roth IRA to retire from. There should be other accounts especially if you start investing at a later age. Always always *always* find an expert to help you out calculate your plans for retirement, focusing on the lifestyle that you have right now and how your lifestyle is going to be projected in the next 10, 15, 20, 30, 40 years from now.

Taxes: contribution to state revenue eleven by the government on workers income and business profits or added to the cost of some goods services and transactions taxes are a mandatory contribution livid on individuals or corporations by the government entity whether local, regional or national.

3

Debt

D EBT: it is an obligation that requires one party the debtor to pay money or other agreed upon value to another party the creditors. ("Debt - Wikipedia") The most common forms of debt are loans including mortgage auto loans, personal loans and credit card debt. Unfortunately, there is an interest charge. This amount varies depending on the bank or the lender. It can be as low as 2.00 % this will be more for a house loan or car loan, then to up to 29% in certain credit cards or banks.

Types of debt:

- Secured debt: this type of debt is usually granted by a bank or lender company using a collateral to be property or asset with a large enough value to cover the amount of debt. Examples that it can be used as collateral vehicles houses boats securities and investments.
- Unsecured debt: this type of debt does not require collateral as security. The ability to repay is reviewed before consideration is given. Since no collateral assignment is issued, the debtor's credit

profile is the primary factor used in deciding whether to approve or deny lending.

- Revolving debt: this debt is a line of credit or an amount that a borrower can continuously borrow from. ("Debt Definition - Investopedia") In other words, the borrower may use funds after a certain amount, pay it back, and borrow up to the amount again.
- Mortgages: a mortgage is a debt issue to purchase real estate such as a house or condominium. It is a form of secure debt as the subject real estate is used as collateral against the loan.
- Corporate Debt: In addition to loans and credit cards debt, companies that need to borrow funds have other debt options: bonds and commercial paper are common types of corporate debt that are not available to individuals.

All this information can be found online *Investopedia.com*. Google research for more detailed information, examples, and explanations.

4

Story

This is the story of Alicia, a 34-year-old woman that has made every and all financial mistakes because she was ignoring the importance of these vocabulary words. She has faced her financial reality and it was worse than an ice shower. Alicia started her working career at 19 years old at a hospital as a CNA. She was making minimum wages but that was OK because that was the beginning of her career. She was happy that she was starting to bring money home and be able to pay for her own expenses. Also, she started buying expensive clothes, shoes and having no control over her money. She was powerful because she had money in her pocket. Unfortunately, she was completely ignoring the opportunity to accumulate wealth to start investing, to start compounding her finances but this never occurred to her. Alicia ignored the importance of the financial future; instead, just spent every single penny because she knew that if she were showing up to work every two weeks, she would receive money again. Also, she was picking up extra shifts and by doing so she was starting a bad habit of putting her time for money. She did not realize the important concept of not trading your time for money until 15 years later.

Alicia got married at 21, she had two kids, her husband and herself kept working increasing their income every single year but still making financial mistakes not saving, not looking ahead increasing expenses at a faster rate than income. Never occurred to them to talk to a financial advisor. A few years later they had to go through the process of buying a home. This took a couple of years of setbacks because they were not prepared. They did not know what it takes to buy a house. They ignored the most important concept which was credit scores. Because of their unhealthy habits of spending more than what they were making with the use of credit cards, they were getting into more and more debt. In consequence their credit scores were in the red, this made the process of buying a house much harder and more expensive because their scores were showing considerable risk borrowers. After Alicia and her husband were denied a couple of times, they were finally able to buy their house. All these years and the lack of knowledge and lack of financial literacy had put this family in jeopardy. In Alicia's head if she and her husband were working, they could pay off debt. In fact, the banks will do the math to make sure they landed them enough money to sink them in debt but not drown them. It is not the bank's fault Alicia understands this concept it is her own fault for not understanding the big business behind loans, she continues to make the mistake of borrowing money from the bank spending more than what she makes to live above means and thinking that she was doing the right thing. Alicia and her husband were making more money every year but having barely anything at the end of the year. At this point in their life all they knew was to show up to work every day and work as much as they could, even extra hours without realizing that they were sacrificing the biggest asset in life which is TIME.

Financially speaking, on average, people are familiar with having a job, working for eight, ten, twelve and sometimes 16 hours a day. That is no joke Alicia worked 16 hour shifts many times. Unfortunately, she thought that by doing so it would bring her wealth. A full-time job and a salary gave her stability knowing that she was providing for her family, but not knowing that this was only one ridiculously small piece of the financial freedom puzzle. Alicia has been giving away the most important asset that she and the rest of the people in this world have in life which is time. Alicia felt fulfilled with her role as wife and mother, that she did not see and worried too much about the financial aspect of her life. Primarily, because both her and her husband were providing paychecks every two weeks which allowed them to make it month to month and save a portion of the money but not a lot because they were paying debt. Both Alicia and her husband's solid jobs gave them reassurance that not everything was done wrong. With Alicia's level of education, she had moved up the ladder in her job. These were big accomplishments for her until she reached the cap of what she can make. And why this was such a significant impact for Alicia was because her wealth is based on what she makes at her job and that's IT. In these years with inflation and the changes that are happening in the world Alicia recognizes that this is not enough to support herself and her family neither will this work for their future.

5

Realization

Alicia's life changed when she realized that 15 years of her life had passed, and she had only a thousand dollars in the bank. Throughout these years she has bought a couple of cars by obtaining a car loan after a car loan. She manages to pay them off but one way or the other she continues in debt. Because of her uncontrolled and unplanned living expenses she was getting out of one debt and entering a new one. To Alicia's experience all she knew was how to make the money, so she continued borrowing money and making payments. "Buy now to pay later they say." That is an expensive and dangerous way of living. This is a true story of Alicia for the past 15 years making mistake after mistake and finally this last year she came across a video on YouTube about real estate and a recommendation to read Rich Dad Poor Dad.

Which is a book that I highly recommend if you know nothing about financial education. It talks about the concept of working for yourself not for the money. This was Alicia's very first book about finances, she listened to it as an audiobook. She finished the whole book in one sitting then she listened to it again, she could not believe the volume of information that she was obtaining.

Regrets, impotence, and frustration to mention a few of the feelings that Alicia felt after she realized that a lot of time has gone by and the ability to multiply money has gone a little bit out of her hands. it is hard to get out of that thinking and there is a constant push back from her own brain "life is a bitch" but it can only be bad until you let it be bad. Alicia has gained knowledge now; she is acting and in control of her finances. Once she discovered how wrong she was managing her finances and how little or no control over her budget, she acted and started watching YouTube videos and building a financial plan. She for the last year has been reading books and growing her knowledge of financial independence every single day.

After reading the book "Rich Dad Poor Dad" Alicia realized that having her own home was not an investment but a liability, until she does something with her home that could bring her money. This concept can be argued because if she did not have a house, she would have to pay rent which means she would be paying somebody else's mortgage. And that is the TRICK with real estate, whomever is the owner of the property and rents it out it brings cash flow to the owner, this is another topic from the book recognizing the financial concept and the monetary opportunities. Alicia felt her heart racing, It was a cold shower; it was a nice pleasant cold shower that woke her up to reality and opened her brain to a whole new bucket of opportunities in Real State. She did not learn everything from that book, it has been the key that opened her mind to what she believes is going to bring her wealth.

It is important to say that Alicia's job has been very meaningful and rewarding. She has a respectable job, do not take her wrong. But she also recognizes that this job is not enough to accomplish her financial goals. She unfortunately did not even know what her financial goals were or where they needed to be to have a successful longevity. Now Alicia realizes that all these financial steps were simple steps to daily living, that with a little knowledge and adjustments to her life this would have given her a more prosperous future. She is figuring out ways to have money work for her not her for the money, she is currently working on a few strategies to have cash flow and passive income.

6

Vocabulary

C ashflow cash flow refers to the net amount of cash and cash equivalent transferred into and out of a company. Cash flow is the amount of cash that comes in and goes out of a company. Businesses take in money from sales as revenues and spend money on expenses. ("Cash Flow: What It Is, How It Works, and How to Analyze It - Investopedia") They may also receive income from interest, investments, royalties, and licensing agreements and sell products on credit expecting to receive the cash owed at the late date.

Investing: expand money with that expectation of achieving a profit or material result by putting it into financial plans shares or property or by using it to develop a commercial venture ("10 Different Ways to Start Investing with Just $1,000") ("expend money with the expectation of achieving a profit or material …")

The best way to invest is with compound interest just like Albert Einstein said compound interest is the eighth wonder of the world. People who don't understand that they pay it.

Real Estate is a form of real property meaning that is something you own that is attached to a piece of land it can be used for residential commercial or industrial purposes ("What is Real Estate | Bankrate")

Real estate is what the majority of rich people if not all rich people in the world use their money to leverage their investment. There are many books out there that talk about real estate and its benefits. This is a subject that is worth the time to study and understand the benefits of real estate.

Assets are something containing an economic value and or future benefit. An asset can often generate cash flows in the future, such as a piece of machinery, a financial security, or a patent. Personal assets may include a house, car, investments, artwork, or Home Goods ("What Is an Asset? Personal and Business Assets - Investopedia")

Net worth net worth is the value of all your assets minus the total of all your liabilities in other words it is what you own minus what you owe. ("What Is Your Net Worth? - Ramsey - Ramsey Solutions")

Capital this typically cash or liquid assets have been held or obtained for expenditures. wealth in the form of money or other assets owned by a person or organization.

Passive income is unearned income that is acquired automatically with minimal labor to earn or maintain. It is often combined with another source of income such as a side job in the United States, the IRS divides income into three categories: active income passive income and portfolio income. ("Passive income - Wikipedia")

Active income active income refers to money received for performing a service. Wages tips salaries commissions and money from businesses in which there is a material participation.

Portfolio a range of investments held by a person or organization is a collection of financial investments like stocks bonds commodities cash and cash equivalents including clothes and funds in exchange trading funds (ETFs). ("Arya Software | Products | Portfolio, Selection") A person that owns real estate and holds this type of investment it is also included in a portfolio, this is call diversification.

Diversification is a strategy that mixes a wide variety of investments within a portfolio in an attempt to reduce portfolio risks you will often hear people say do not put all your eggs in one basket this in a financial vocabulary means that you're not going to invest all your money into one subject diversifying is the best way to optimize earnings and to avoid big losses.

Liabilities: liabilities the definition of liability the state of being responsible for something especially by law. A thing for which someone is responsible like debt or financial obligations.

7

Interest & Credit

"**I**nterest the proportion of a loan that is charged as interest to the borrower typically expressed as an annual percentage of the loan outstanding." highly encouraging the readers to understand interest rates especially at times to open credit cards. when purchasing a house or a car the amount of interest rates Are calculated differently this type of loans are called amortization loans which means you have a period of time to pay for which they calculate the amount of money being borrowed times the interest they calculate that for the number of months the loan is being round 10 and the barrier is paying the bank interest rate on the principle remaining balance.

- The interest rate is the amount charged on top of the principle by a lender to a borrower for the use of assets ("Interest Rates: Different Types and What They Mean to Borrowers")
- An interest rate also applies to the amount earned at a bank or credit union from a deposit account
- A borrower is considering lower risk by the lender and will have a lower interest rate. A loan that is consider elevated risk will have a higher interest rate. ("What is Interest rate? Interest rate definition

encyclopedia")

- The APR is the interest rate that is earned at a bank or credit union from a savings account or a CD savings account in series use compound interest
  - Simple interest these are used most for home loans and car loans
  - Compound interest is used more for credit cards and certain high-risk loans.

It is crucial to understand interest rates when you are borrowing money from a bank or an institution. Consider the pros and the cons about asking for a certain amount of money and what is going to be used for

Credit meaning of credit the definition of credit the ability of a customer to obtain goods or services before payment based on the trust that payment will be made in the future.

Credit score meaning Consumer Financial Protection Bureau a credit score is a prediction of your credit behavior such as how likely you are to pay a loan back on time based on information from your credit reports. In the United States credit scores are a major number and factor to consider when an individual is buying a house, car and/or applying for a credit card. If you don't have a good credit score, which could be from 650 to be considered somewhat OK to 700-800 banks will lend you money based on those scores. Banks will decide if you are low-risk or a high-risk individual after analyzing the credit report. Also, credit score will determine the interest rates that the bank will offer. If a person is considered high-risk that person will get a higher interest rate, consequently this individual will end up with a very expensive debt.

8

Mindset

There are YouTube videos and books that taught Alicia the concepts of self-talk, motivation, and discipline. One of the biggest things that she learned from all this was to reset the brain and correct the mindset to fulfill herself first before fulfilling others. Now Alicia's future is going to be different than what she was projecting before she had awareness of financial education. What she did not know 15 years ago is not going to stop her now because she knows what needs to be done, she knows how to start investing, she knows how to build a budget and she knows what a liability is.

Alicia has learned this past year to be ahead and start investing at a younger age. The money invested will multiply, triplicate, or even quadruplicate if people start as early as 18 years of age. The purpose of this book is to scream a big wake up call to the people that are reading this content. Is not a coincidence that you have made it this far. You are working on your personal growth just like Alicia did. And to be all transparent she still has a way to go but she understands that she must start somewhere. She also recognizes that school is important, but these vocabulary words are also important. They will make a whole life difference when put into practice because developing financial literacy is as important as a four-year degree. Statistics show that people get out of school and do not have the job that they deserve. After all the demanding work and time that they had put into their education, the beginning can be difficult, and people find themselves lost or broke. That is why before starting a life time journey of education, it's critical to have a financial plan and a vision of where you see your self in the future.

Alicia has been studying what rich people do to grow their wealth. She understands that everything starts in the brain with the correct mindset and with a clear plan, as she has been watching YouTube videos, googling keywords, studying biographies of successful people, and listening to audiobooks like this one. Alicia has gathered the inspiration to continue learning and investing the time to learn more. She has yet to discover the path, but she knows she is in the right direction. At times from reading multiple books, it feels like they are all the same in different words, but what Alicia has discovered is that yes, the information is the same because the principles of success are all the same. What makes it different is how everyone understands the concept and puts it to work to help everyone's wealth.

9

Conclusion

To conclude this book, I would like to thank all and every single one of you for taking the time to read this book. This is a small and not professionally written book, but it has a big purpose. Alicia wants to give everybody a message to please be aware of your finances as soon as possible. Understand the importance of time for money and that as one source of income is not enough to retire with dignity at an early age. Alicia's journey just began in 2022 at 34 years of age, she will be applying all the words that she just shares in this book, and she will have more to bring out in the future as she grows her own wealth. Thank you so much again for your time and if this book helps you at all or if you are interested to see Alicia's growth all we ask for is to leave us a brief review on Amazon or at the cite where you perched this book, and by doing so it will help the author improve the work.

10

Resources

Interest Rates: Different Types and What They Mean to Borrowers. (2022, July 6). Investopedia. https://www.investopedia.com/terms/i/interestrate.asp

Wikipedia contributors. (2023a, February 3). *Passive income.* Wikipedia. https://en.m.wikipedia.org/wiki/Passive_income
    Captcha Challenge. . . . (n.d.). https://quizlet.com/178284631/investing-unit-vocabulary-flash-cards/
    Beck, R. H. (2022, September 16). *What is real estate?* Bankrate. Retrieved February 5, 2023, from https://www.bankrate.com/real-estate/what-is-real-estate/
    Page Not Found. (n.d.). Investopedia. Retrieved February 7, 2023, from https://www.investopedia.com/terms/i/income
    Ramsey Solutions. (n.d.). *Page Not Found | RamseySolutions.com.* Retrieved February 15, 2023, from https://www.ramseysolutions.com/net+worth